Rusty's Song

by Milo Mason

Grounding Grandma

by Sharon Fear

Robo-Police

by Meish Goldish

MODERN CURRICULUM PRESS

Pearson Learning Group

ISBN 1-4284-0401-5

Printed in the United States of America

3 4 5 6 7 8 9 10   10 09 08

Pearson Learning Group

1-800-321-3106
www.pearsonlearning.com

Stories to Make You Laugh

Contents

RUSTY'S SONG

by Milo Mason

illustrated by Lee Lee Brazeal

This is a story about two friends named Rusty and the Old Cowboy.

Rusty was called Rusty because her fur was the color of a rusty nail.

The Old Cowboy was called the Old Cowboy because that's exactly what he was.

The Old Cowboy and Rusty had a good life. They just drifted here and there, looking at the scenery. At night by the campfire, Rusty would doze while the Old Cowboy wrote in his diary.

That diary must have held all the Old Cowboy's thoughts and dreams. He didn't talk and never had. Not a word. And no one knew why.

Rusty didn't talk either, but what would you expect from a dog? What Rusty could do, though, was better than talking.

Rusty could sing. She didn't sing words, of course, but it was amazing what that dog could do with yelps, howls, and whines. Why, Rusty sang so well she sounded almost human—only better.

Her singing was soft and gentle. It drifted to you like a cloud. All of Rusty's songs were sad, but that's the way a cowboy likes his singing—sad.

It was strange. But Rusty's singing always made her old pal happy.

The Old Cowboy and Rusty never had much money. You don't need much when you sleep under the stars and all you eat is beans.

But even beans cost something. And when the money ran out, they couldn't buy more. The first day wasn't so bad. Anybody can go a day without food. The day after that was okay too.

By the third day, though, they were feeling bad. They needed money and they needed money right away.

Then the Old Cowboy saw a sign. The town was holding a singing cowboy contest. First prize was one hundred dollars. That sign triggered an idea in the Old Cowboy's head. He studied it for a long time. Then he studied Rusty.

Before long, he had a plan. He was determined to win that contest money.

Singing
Cowboy
Contest
Today!!!
First Prize
$100

Sometimes plans don't work out. The contest judge shook his head.

"No dogs allowed!" he said. "This here's a singing cowboy contest, not a singing cow*dog* contest."

The Old Cowboy wanted to say that wasn't fair. He wanted to say a cowdog is as good as a cowboy. He wanted to say it's the singing that counts.

But of course he didn't say a thing. He never did.

The Old Cowboy figured he had no other choice. He signed himself up for the contest.

The judge said, "Old Cowboy, how are you going to sing? You can't even talk!"

The Old Cowboy just looked at the judge and didn't say a word.

The contest was that very night. Too soon, it was the Old Cowboy's turn to sing.

His hands began to tremble.

His knees began to knock.

He walked out onto the stage.

Someone hit a switch and the spotlight came on.

The crowd waited. The Old Cowboy looked horrified, but he opened his mouth to sing. The audience leaned forward.

What happened next was awful. Nothing came out of the Old Cowboy's mouth. Not so much as a peep! He tried and tried, but he just couldn't squeeze out a sound.

The audience began to laugh. Then they began to boo.

The Old Cowboy shut his mouth. He hung his head. Rusty hated to see her friend unhappy. So she did the only thing she could to make him feel better.

Rusty started singing.

As soon as they heard Rusty's song, the crowd fell silent. It was just as though someone had flipped a switch. No one coughed, sneezed, or moved.

Rusty sang the saddest song she knew. She sang it better than she had ever sung before. Her song soared out of her throat and drifted over the audience. It was the prettiest song anyone had ever heard.

Rusty's song was so sad and pretty it made everyone in town want to cry. That cowdog song just triggered something in them. It was a sight to see. Grown men's lips began to tremble. Rusty sang louder. Then the crowd started to bawl like babies.

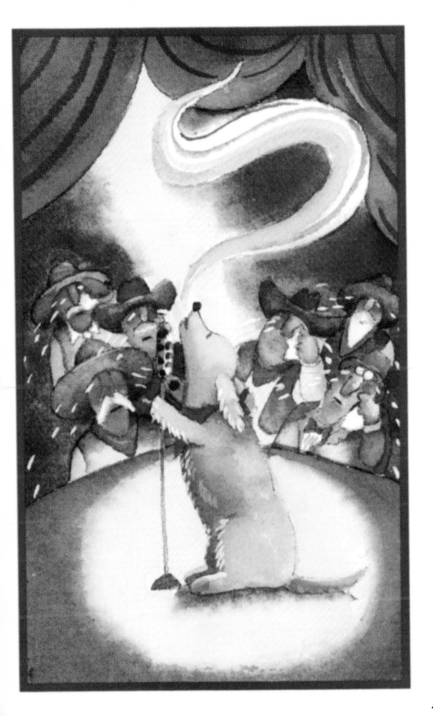

13

When Rusty finished, all
the folks jumped to their feet
and cheered.

The Old Cowboy grinned from
ear to ear. He clapped until his
hands were sore. Then he gave that
dog a big old hug.

The judge wiped his eyes and
blew his nose.

"Well," he said, "maybe it's
against the rules, but so what? Who
cares if you're a cowdog instead of a
cowboy? If you sing as well as that,
it doesn't matter a lick if you're
an elephant! Rusty, you win
first prize!"

Rusty and the Old Cowboy did their shopping, and then they drifted out of town. The Old Cowboy had a wonderful new tale to write in his diary that night. And if he was happy, Rusty was happy too.

Life was looking mighty fine.

A hundred dollars can buy a lot of beans.

GROUNDING GRANDMA

by Sharon Fear
illustrated by Margeaux Lucas

His mother, his father, and his sister were at the kitchen table when Burt came in. They looked so serious that, on his own, he stopped slam-bamming his basketball on the kitchen floor. It was something his mother was always telling him not to do.

"What's up?" he asked.

"We've had a letter from Mount Airy," said his mother. "Mr. and Mrs. Mason, your grandmother's neighbors, sent it."

The Masons were just two of the neighborhood volunteers who looked in on Grandma Wingfield, now that she was getting older and lived alone. The volunteers sent a monthly letter detailing Grandma's condition, which, up to now, had been fine.

"Grandma isn't sick, is she?" asked Burt.

"No, no," said Mr. Wingfield. And then he read what Mrs. Mason had written.

Physically she is fine. But she does seem to forget that she can't do all the things she used to. She forgets to be careful about going up on ladders and such.

Burt saw his sister grin behind her hand. But before he could ask what was so funny, his mother continued.

"Connie Mason isn't the hysterical type," she said. "If she thinks there's cause to worry, there probably is. So we're all driving to Mount Airy this weekend to make sure Grandma is all right. And, Burt, I want you and Carol to stay for the week. It's good you have a week off from school. Your Dad and I have to come back to work, but we'll come back up on the next weekend."

"Oh, Mom," said Burt, unable to keep the whine out of his voice. "I wanted to work on my dribbling and shooting this week."

"There's a hoop on Grandma's barn," said his dad.

"Did you ever try dribbling in dirt?" Burt shot back.

"It will be fine," said Carol. "I'll work with you."

Three years older and a foot taller, his sister Carol had an almost miraculous vertical leap. Burt had to admit, he could learn a lot of basketball from her.

"OK, OK," he said, "to Grandmother's house we go."

Mount Airy was small, rural, and well off the main roads. The weather vanes that topped so many barns and houses gave the place an antique look.

Burt noticed a red windsock billowing stiffly above the trees in the distance. "Is there an airport around here?" he asked.

"I don't think so," said his father.

From the roof of a barn, a white-haired man in overalls stopped his hammering to wave.

"That guy is pretty old!" said Burt. "He'd better watch his step."

"That's a cousin of yours. Another Wingfield," said his mother, as if it were the answer to a question.

At Grandma's house they knocked and waited, knocked and waited, for almost two minutes.

When at last Grandma came, she was patting her chest, out of breath. "Sorry it took me so long to answer the door. I was up ... stairs. Upstairs."

And she looked Burt right in the eye and gave him one of those bland, unreadable looks that often seemed to mask her face.

But then she recovered, kissed her son and his wife, and told the children how they'd grown. Finally she invited everybody in.

Over the next few days, between basketball practice and chores, Burt kept an eye on Grandma, as his parents had asked. She seemed OK to him. He saw no extreme forgetfulness and no bizarre behavior—until he found her on the roof of the old shed.

"Grandma! You shouldn't be up there! Let me help you down. Be careful!"

"Oh, Burt, honey, thank goodness you're here. I just got up to check that leak in the roof, and my ladder fell down. It's over there somewhere."

He found it in the grass, pretty far from the shed. And when he helped her down, he was almost shaking at the thought of what might have happened to this frail old lady.

But that notion didn't last long.

The next day, after watching Burt and Carol dribbling and shooting hoops for a while, Grandma stepped in, stole the ball, put it in the dirt once, and went to the hoop like a pro.

"Grandma!" Burt shouted. "You dunked! You dunked! You dunked!" He felt stupid saying it over and over, but that was the only thought in his head, and those were the only words: "You dunked!"

In bed that night he pondered this event. True, Grandma was quite tall. The whole family was taller than average. And, true, she had been remarkably athletic her whole life. He knew she skied in her younger days. She had been a good swimmer and an excellent diver.

So she was tall. So she skied, swam, and dived. So what? She was in her seventies! And she dunked! And what was she doing climbing on that roof at her age? He thought of that other old person, "another Wingfield," on a roof.

And windsocks.

And weather vanes.

And he went to sleep with the sound of wind in his ears.

In the morning he was momentarily relieved to find Grandma doing ordinary, grandmotherly things. She had her feather duster out and was vigorously knocking cobwebs out of one corner of the living room.

The only thing was, it was a corner up at the ceiling. And as he stepped past the tall, wing-backed chair, Burt realized she wasn't standing on anything.

When she heard him gasp, she turned around slowly in the air and began to descend.

He turned around slowly too—and fainted.

Explanations were not enough. Only demonstrations convinced Burt that what he had seen was true.

"You can fly," he said. "You . . . can . . . fly."

"Most of the Wingfields around here can," said Grandma. "Those who can't are willing to keep our little secret. Anyway, who would believe them if they told?"

"All those weather vanes," Burt said. "And every time we came to town, somebody was fixing his roof. I knew something was up."

Grandma laughed at his choice of words.

"We're often up," said Grandma. "But if a stranger comes through, we pretend to be fixing the roof. We're supposed to keep ladders leaning against our outbuildings, to make it look as if that's how we got up.

"But that day I forgot my ladder. And, today ... oh, Burt! I'm so sorry I frightened you that way! Maybe I am getting forgetful. Maybe it is time I was grounded."

"Can Dad fly?" Burt asked.

"Perhaps he can," said Grandma. "But he never wanted to. Maybe he never tried. I know he doesn't like to talk about it."

"But you can, can't you?" he said to Carol. "That's why your jump shot is so good."

"Well," she said, "the jump part is easy, but I still have to practice the shot."

He was almost afraid to ask the next, the obvious, question. "What about . . . I mean, can I?"

"If you have inherited our peculiar family trait," said Grandma, "it should show up anytime now."

"Outstanding!" he cried. "I could slam dunk! No one could guard me! I could sail right over anyone!"

"Yes, you could," said Grandma. "But, of course, that would be cheating."

All three were quiet while Burt considered her words.

Then they talked it over and decided a couple of things. First, the children would spend the summer at Grandma's, helping her decide if she really was becoming forgetful. Second, if Burt showed signs of inheriting the family trait, he must be taught the rules of flying.

Everybody was satisfied with those decisions.

And by the end of summer they would know.

They would know whether Grandma Wingfield should be grounded, and whether Burt Wingfield would get his wings.

Robo-Police

by Meish Goldish
illustrated by Debbie Tilley

ROBO-POLICE

"This place is a mess!"

Carla had to raise her voice to be heard over the noontime racket.

Juan looked around and saw that Carla was right. The school cafeteria was indeed a mess. On the floor were straws, wrappers, napkins, paper cups, crumbs, and spilled milk.

"It looks like a tornado hit here," Carla said as she wrinkled her nose. "I feel sorry for the custodian who has to clean it up."

"Kids hurry too much when they empty their trays," Juan said.

"This cafeteria is just too big for only a few teachers to police," Carla said.

When Juan heard the word *police*, his eyes lit up. "Carla, you just gave me a great idea!" he said. "Come to my house after school."

Juan jumped up and began to leave.

"Hey, Juan!" Carla called. "Dump your tray!"

"Oops!" said Juan, with a red face.

After school, Carla went over to Juan's house.

"So what's this brilliant idea of yours?" she asked.

"Did you ever see that movie about a robot police officer?" Juan asked. Carla shook her head no.

"Well," Juan said, "I was thinking we could have a robot police the cafeteria to get kids to clean up the messes they make."

Carla gave Juan a funny look. "I think you've seen one too many robot movies!" she teased.

"Just come with me," Juan said. "It's time for a demonstration," he added as he led the way to the basement.

"What's this?" Carla asked.

"It's my father's workshop," Juan explained. "He keeps some cool equipment down here, including this."

"A vacuum cleaner?" Carla asked.

"It's not an ordinary vacuum cleaner," Juan said. "This is a super vac. It can pick up big messes like wood chips, paper, and even spilled milk! Watch, as the demonstration begins!"

First Juan tipped over a garbage can. Then he turned on the vacuum, which made a loud racket as Juan ran it along the floor. In a short time, the entire mess from the garbage can had disappeared.

Juan turned off the machine.

"That's quite a cleaner," Carla said, "but how could we use it in the school cafeteria?"

"Look at this," Juan said with a determined look on his face.

"Meet Robo-Police," Juan said.

Carla stared at the invention. The robot had a sign on its front.

It said:

I AM THE ROBO-POLICE.

FEED ME.

(I EAT WITH MY FEET.)

Carla laughed. "I like it," she said, "but how does it work?"

"Easy," Juan explained. "I turn on the robot, and it goes from table to table, eating the trash on the floor."

"But how does it stop and go?" Carla asked. "Do you stay inside the box to push it?"

"Oh," Juan said, "I never thought about that."

Juan and Carla went back upstairs. Suddenly, Carla had an idea.

"My brother has an electric car," she said. "It moves by remote control. Maybe you could make the vacuum cleaner work by remote control too."

"Great idea!" Juan cried. "My father could help me hook it up. Carla, you're a genius!"

A few days later, Juan told Carla that the invention was ready.

"I hooked up the robot with remote buttons," he said. "It's so cool now, because I can make the robot stop, go, and turn. My father says I can take it to school for a few days."

"When will we get to see it work?" Carla asked.

"I told Ms. Jones about it," Juan said. "She said we could give a demonstration at lunch tomorrow."

"We?" asked Carla.

"Sure! You helped me invent it," Juan told her.

The next morning, Juan's father drove the robot to school. It stayed in the principal's office until it was lunchtime. Then Juan and Carla rolled it to the cafeteria as Juan smiled with happy anticipation. Ms. Jones went along to watch the demonstration.

I AM THE ROBO-POLICE. FEED ME. (I EAT WITH MY FEET.)

The cafeteria was messy, as usual.

The robot began to make its usual loud racket as it rolled to the first table and stopped. All the students got quiet. They read the sign on the robot.

Then the robot went right to work. In no time, the straws and wrappers were gone from the floor, and so were the food spills. The students all cheered.

"Go, Robo!" they cried. "Eat with your feet!"

Juan pressed the remote again, and the demonstration continued. Robo made its way to the next table. Just as before, it cleaned the floor in no time. The students cheered again. The same thing happened at table after table.

Then something strange happened. Robo stopped at a table where some students were still eating. It stood still for a minute, and then it cleaned one student's lunch right off the table.

"Uh oh!" said Juan.

Robo just kept going, grabbing one boy's sandwich right out of his hands!

Juan rushed to turn Robo off.

51

Finally, Robo stopped. Juan and Carla looked at each other.

"Well, maybe Robo needs a little more work," said Carla. "Robo isn't quite ready for cleaning up the cafeteria just yet."

"Yes, I guess we'll just have to clean up our own messes," Juan said, laughing.